Aboriginal American Slaves and Their Problem

Presented by

Meru El Muad'Dib

1828 Definition of American

AMER'ICAN, noun A native of America; **originally applied to the aboriginals, or copper-colored races**, found here by the Europeans; but now applied to the descendants of Europeans born in America.

The word Indian is a misnomer. The people of this land did not call themselves Indians. That is a label placed upon them by Europeans. So when you see the words, **Indian, Negro, colored, African American, black** or any other label, please understand that I am referring to the Aboriginal American.

The Other Slave Trade

Most Americans believe the first slaves arrived in America in 1619 at Jamestown, Virginia. Most are not aware that slavery was already taking place in America. It started over one-hundred years earlier with Christopher Columbus. Let's take a look…

In any case, Americans did not reach Europe and Africa solely by means of voluntary or storm-driven adventures. European expeditions to the America's are known to have taken thousands of Americans to the east, and some of these involuntary journeys preceded the time of Columbus. Pg 18

In any case, by the 1490's Americans were appearing once again in European cities. Although Terranova (Newfoundland) and Greenland continued to be a source of captives from 1501 on, it is best at this point to turn away from northern waters to examine the activities of Columbus and the catastrophic slave trade in American flesh which he initiated in the Caribbean region. Pg 21

Moreover, Columbus' impact was singular in that he was, from the first, a dedicated slaver and exploiter with an extremely callous and indifferent attitude towards culturally different human beings. Pg 22

Columbus on his first voyage kidnapped at least 27 Americans, two of whom escaped, leaving a total of 25 in his hands. His attitude is expressed as follows, when, after abducting seven males, he says: 'when your highness so command, they can all be carried off to Castille or held captive in the island itself, since with fifty men they would be all kept in subjection and forced to do whatever may be wished.' Thus, at the very first island reached (Guanani), Columbus already was able to express his willingness to depopulate the entire island in order that the Americans might be sold as slaves in Europe, **or held as captives**, **in their own land**. Pg 22

Remember Martin Luther King Jr. said, in his March On Washington speech, "One hundred years later, the Negro is still languishing in the corners of American society and finds himself **an exile in his own land**. So we have come here today to dramatize a shameful condition."

After two boys escaped, Columbus stated: 'and I have no great confidence in them, because many times they have attempted to escape.' His philosophy of conquest and colonialism was extremely well developed: "And they are fitted to be ruled and to be set to work, to cultivate the land and to do all else that may be necessary, and you may build towns and teach them to go clothed and to adopt our customs.' Also: they would make good industrious servants.' Pg 22

While still at sea, on his first voyage, Columbus advocated the capture of Caribs: 'very fierce people and well proportioned and of very good understanding, who, after being removed from their inhumanity, we believe will be better than any other slaves whatsoever.' On January 30, 1494 he addressed to the Spanish monarchs a plan for sending men, women, and children to Spain to learn the Castillian language and to be trained in service, with more care ‘than other slaves’ receive, saying that this plan would save a great number of souls while at the same time providing the colonizing Spaniards with the profit needed to supply themselves with goods. In other words, Columbus proposed (after his first voyage) that American slavery be used to finance the conquest. Pg 22

Subsequently, Columbus began to enslave Taino (Arawak) people who were definitely not cannibalistic and it would appear that the idea of punishing Caribs (for being allegedly so) was simply as expedient financial strategy. Pg 23

Thus Columbus, according to las Casas, was determined to ‘consume’ the entire population of Haiti by filling every ship with slaves to be sold in the Canary, Azores and Cabo Verde islands or wherever, and planned that these slaves would finance the conquest.

As Las Casas points out, for Columbus the lives of Americans were obviously ‘nothing’ and the continuous wars to obtain slaves were simply necessary to fill the ships.

Thus, even as Columbus was loading five ships with slaves, he was proposing to sell 4,000 in various parts of the Mediterranean and along the coast of Africa.

Columbus was also unconcerned that many Americans would die in the slave trade because, as he said, the blacks and the native Canary Islanders when first enslaved also died in great numbers.

The shipment of Americans to Europe and Africa by Columbus (and by other Spaniards) was, then, not an accident, nor was it a result of armed resistance or alleged cannibalism.

What was the result? First, many thousands of Americans were shipped to Spain during Columbus' period of dominance in the Caribbean. It is difficult to calculate the exact number because many ships departed from Haiti without leaving any record of their cargo, but we may be sure that they did not leave empty.

In any case, at least 3,000 Americans are known to have been shipped to Europe between 1493 and 1501, with the likely total being possibly double that. Most were sent to the Seville area, where they seem to show up in the slave markets as negros without a place of origin being mentioned.

Columbus reached Lisbon in early March 1493. Many people came to see the captive Americans and it is very likely that some of the latter were taken nine leagues into the interior to see the king of Portugal.

Shortly thereafter some of the Americans were taken to Seville, perhaps seven to ten being still alive and together. Some were left in that area, while about six or seven were taken overland across Spain to Barcelona where they were displayed before the monarchs in mid-April.

But the tens of millions of Americans who disappeared after 1492 did not all die in the 'holocaust' inflicted within the Americas. Many thousands were sent to Europe and Africa where their descendants still live. Pag 23-25 from:

Africans and Native Americans: The Language of Race and the Evolution of Red-Black Peoples by Jack D. Forbes

Textbooks and classroom lesson plans are starting to present a more clear-eyed view of America's history—such as slowly recognizing the violence that happened when European settlers encountered the indigenous people of the so-called "New World." But there are still many overlooked stories. One of these startling omissions to the history books is something Margaret Ellen Newell is calling attention to in her book, Brethren by Nature: **Colonists living in New England relied on the labor of thousands of Native Americans** to build their new lives.

The enslavement of New England's indigenous people was glossed over in the work of historians after World War I, Newell says, as Tanya H. Lee reports for Indian Country Today. Newell, an associate professor of history at Ohio State University, writes that historians "**reconstructed the compelling narrative of the Puritan migration**.... Many of these works stressed the uniqueness of New England culture and sought there the origins of American exceptionalism."

During the course of researching her first book, From Dependency to Independence: Economic Revolution in Colonial New England, **Newell came across a list of Native American slaves kept by colonists in the Massachusetts Bay Colony**. She was surprised by the find because **she had been taught that New England colonists didn't keep Native Americans as slaves**, because they often ran away. But **that impression was incorrect**.

Lee writes:

*The colonial economy depended on slavery, many well-to-do households functioned only because of slavery, early colonial legal codes were devised to justify slavery and the **Pequot War and King Philip's War were fought in large measure to perpetuate slavery.***

Indeed, in the 1630s, the Connecticut River Valley was home to the powerful Pequots. The settlers at Plymouth and Massachusetts Bay wanted their rich, fertile land and in order to get it, they persuaded Mohegan and Narragansett allies to help them fight the Pequots. In 1637, they burned a village on the banks of the Mystic River in southeastern Connecticut, killing 400 to 700 Pequots, according to the Society of Colonial Wars in the State of Connecticut. That massacre turned the tide of the war and Pequot survivors were pursued, captured and **sold as slaves**.

King Philip's War in the mid 1670s—which was fought to protest the English colonists encroaching influence and forced labor of Native Americans—ended with "**as many as 40 percent of the Indians in southern New England living in English households as indentured servants or slaves**," Lee writes.

The English colonists weren't the only ones to use the labor of enslaved indigenous people, of course. "**The Spanish were almost totally dependent on Indian labor in most of their colonies**," writes Alan Gallay for History Now. **Enslaving Native Americans became one of the primary ways to expand the economy for colonists in South Carolina and to a lesser extent in North Carolina**, **Virginia and Louisiana**. "**From 1670 to 1720 more Indians were shipped out of Charleston, South Carolina, than Africans were imported as slaves**—and Charleston was a major port for bringing in Africans," Gallay writes.

As the African slave trade took off in the late 1700s, the Native American slave trade waned. Many remaining tribes had been pushed West, but something else was taking place, that pushed the data down, as well. Some Native Americans were intermarrying with African American. **The children were then referred to as "colored," effectively erasing their Native American heritage**. The enslavement of Native Americans thus became obscured, but modern DNA technology helped keep that story from being lost to time.

https://www.smithsonianmag.com/smart-news/colonial-america-depended-enslavement-indigenous-people-180957900/

Here are three scenes from the history of slavery in North America. In 1637, a group of Pequot Indians, men and boys, having risen up against English colonists in Connecticut and been defeated, **were sold to plantations in the West Indies** in exchange for African slaves, allowing the colonists to remove a resistant element from their midst. (The tribe's women were pressed into service in white homes in New England, where domestic workers were sorely lacking.) In 1741, **an 800-foot-long coffle of recently enslaved Sioux Indians, procured by a group of Cree, Assiniboine, and Monsoni warriors, arrived in Montreal**, **ready for sale to French colonists hungry for domestic and agricultural labor**.

In recent years, a new wave of historians of American slavery has been directing attention to the ways these sins overlapped. The stories they have uncovered throw African slavery—still the narrative that dominates our national memory—into a different light, revealing that **the seeds of that system were sown in earlier attempts to exploit Native labor**. The record of Native enslavement also shows how the white desire to put workers in bondage intensified the chaos of contact, disrupting intertribal politics and creating uncertainty and instability among people already struggling to adapt to a radically new balance of power.

Before looking at the way Native enslavement happened on the local level (really the only way to approach a history this fragmented and various), it helps to appreciate the sweep of the phenomenon. How common was it for Indians to be enslaved by Euro-Americans? Counting can be difficult, because many instances of Native enslavement in the Colonial period were illegal or ad hoc and left no paper trail. But historians have tried. A few of their estimates: Thousands of Indians were enslaved in Colonial New England, according to Margaret Ellen Newell. Alan Gallay writes that **between 1670 and 1715, more Indians were exported into slavery through Charles Town (now Charleston, South Carolina) than Africans were imported**. Brett Rushforth recently attempted a tally of the total numbers of enslaved, and he told me that he thinks 2 million to 4 million indigenous people in the Americas, North and South, may have been enslaved over the centuries that the practice prevailed—a much larger number than had previously been thought.

...but the earliest history of the European colonies in the Americas is marked by Native bondage. "**If you go up to about 1680 or 1690 there still, by that period, had been more enslaved Indians than enslaved Africans in the Americas**."

The practice dates back to the earliest history of the European colonies in the future United States. Take the example of the Pequot who were enslaved in 1637 after clashing with the English. As Newell writes in a new book, *Brethren by Nature: New England Indians, Colonists, and the Origins of American Slavery*, by the time the ship **Desire transported the defeated Pequot men and boys to the Caribbean**, colonists in New England, desperate for bodies and hands to supplement their own meager workforce, had spent years trying out various strategies of binding Native labor.

During the Pequot War, which was initially instigated by struggles over trade and land among the Europeans, the Pequot, and rival tribes, colonists explicitly named the procurement of captives as one of their goals. **Soldiers sent groups of captured Pequot to Boston and other cities for distribution, while claiming particular captured people as their own**. Soldier Israel

Stoughton wrote to John Winthrop, having sent "48 or 50 women and Children" to the governor to distribute as he pleased:

There is one ... that is the fairest and largest that I saw amongst them to whom I have given a coate to cloath her: It is my desire to have her for a servant ... There is a little Squaw that Stewart Calaot desireth ... Lifetennant Davenport also desireth one, to wit a tall one that hath 3 stroakes upon her stummach ...

A few years after the conclusion of the war, in 1641, the colonists of Massachusetts Bay passed the first formal law regulating slavery in English America, in a section of the longer document known as the Body of Liberties. The section's language allowed enslavement of "those lawfull Captives taken in just warres, and such strangers as willingly selle themselves or are sold to us," and left room for legal bondage of others the authorities might deem enslaved in the future. **The Body of Liberties codified the colonists' possession of Native workers and opened the door for the expansion of African enslavement**.

* * *

Europeans did not introduce slavery to this continent. Many, though not all, of the Native groups in the land that later became the United States and Canada practiced slavery before Europeans arrived. Native tribes, in their diversity, did not have a uniform approach to enslavement (given Americans' propensity to collapse all Native people together, this bears reiterating). Many of those traditions also changed when tribes began to contend with the European presence. "There are many slaveries, and colonialism brings different slaveries into contact with one another," historian Christina Snyder, who wrote a history of Native slavery in the Southeast, told me. Contact pushed Native practices to change over time, as tribes contested, or adapted to, European demands. But, broadly speaking, **Native types of**

enslavement were often about kinship, reproductive labor, and diplomacy, rather than solely the extraction of agricultural or domestic labor. The difference between these slaveries and European bondage of Africans was great.

Historian Pekka Hämäläinen, in his 2009 book The Comanche Empire, writes of Comanche uses of slavery during their period of dominance of the American Southwest between 1750 and 1850. The Comanche exercised hegemony in part by numerical superiority, and enslavement was part of that strategy. Hämäläinen writes that Comanches put captives through a rigorous process of enslavement—a dehumanizing initiation that brought a non-Comanche captive into the tribe through renaming, tattooing, beating, whipping, mutilation, and starvation—but stipulates that once a person was enslaved, there were varying degrees of freedom and privilege she or he could attain. Male captives might be made blood bondsmen with their owners, protecting them from ill treatment and casual sale; women might be married into the tribe, after which time they became, as Hämäläinen puts it, "full-fledged tribal members"; younger, more impressionable children might be adopted outright. After a period of trauma, captives could, quite possibly, attain quasi-free status; their own children would be Comanches.

In his book Bonds of Alliance: Indigenous and Atlantic Slaveries in New France, Brett Rushforth writes about a similar tradition of "natal alienation" practiced by enslaving tribes in the Pays d'en Haut (the French name for the Great Lakes region and the land west of Montreal) in order to strip a captive of his or her old identity and life. Rushforth does not sell short the awfulness of these processes; still, he pointed out: "Rather than a closed slave system designed to move slaves 'up and out'—excluding slaves and their descendants from full participation in their masters' society, even when freed—indigenous slavery moved captives 'up and in' toward full, if forced, assimilation." This was more than Africans enslaved by Europeans could hope for, after the legal codification of hereditary chattel slavery in the 17th and early 18th centuries.

The disconnect between Native uses of slavery and European understandings of the practice often made for miscommunication. In some places, ironically enough, Native groups themselves initiated the trade in captives to the Europeans. In the Pays d'en Haut, Rushforth found in his research, Indian groups believed in "a diplomatic function of captive-taking." Early in their time in the area, French officials found themselves offered Native slaves as tokens of trust, peace, and friendship. "When the French embedded themselves in these Native systems of alliance and trade and diplomacy, they found themselves engaged in these captive exchanges—not unwillingly, of course," Rushforth told me. "At the same time, the French were trading African slaves in the Caribbean and South America, so it's not like the Indians forced this upon the French. The French found the diplomatic function of it to be kind of confusing. They didn't know what to make of it at first, and then they sort of manipulated it to their own advantage."

Rushforth notes that the political equilibrium that prevailed before the arrival of Europeans had kept the Native slave trade minimal. "If you're a Native group in the Midwest and it's hunting season, you have to make a choice," he said. " 'Are we going to go after an enemy, or are we going to stock up on meat and hides and other things?' It's either hunting or captive-raiding. And so that created these disincentives to go after captives, because there were all kinds of reasons you wanted to have peace, all kinds of reasons you wanted to have your economy running."

Soon, however, French officials, desiring more slaves, began to incentivize Native people to take captives by promising desirable goods in return. Nearby tribes began to raid one another in earnest, often venturing far into the interior of the present-day United States to grab Pawnee and other Plains Indians. With French traders now offering goods and comestibles in exchange for captives, the old political balance was disrupted. "If you can go raid your enemies and trade them, for food and cloth and other things, you can actually sort of collapse those two choices into one," Rushforth said. "That means the choice to raid for captives was much less costly for them. And so they actually did it much more often." The French, wanting to be secure from violence in Montreal, made rules that pushed the chaos of raiding farther away—circumscribing the sale of Native slaves from nearby tribes, for example. "So they can create all of this extractive force," Rushforth noted, "and it just makes everything chaotic and destructive out there."

As in the Pays d'en Haut, so in the American South, where the demand for Indian slaves changed the political relationships between tribes. "Once Europeans showed up and they demanded that the supply of Native slaves amp up to meet the demand, Native practices regarding slaves changed," Snyder said. "So people who might once have been adopted or killed now became slaves."

Captives experienced enslavement by 17th-century Europeans in a much different way than enslavement by another Indian tribe. If a Native person was made captive by a rival tribe, a set of relatively predictable traditions governed his or her treatment. But after a Native captor sold a captive to a European, the person was swept into a global system. She, or he, was now a commodity. In the South, Snyder said,

"[Natives] basically became slaves in a really similar way to African slaves, who were also arriving at the same time in South Carolina." Reduced to a source of labor, and caught up in a wide-reaching web of exchange, **the Native slave could be sold very far away**. Rushforth points to **instances of Apaches and other Plains peoples being sold, through Quebec, to the Caribbean. "There were Plains Apaches who showed up on sugar plantations in Martinique**," he said.

While the histories of Native enslavement and enslaving might seem to be separate spheres of study, they too are intertwined. Tribal groups could find themselves shifting from enslavers to enslaved, as their relationships to Euro-Americans, and with other tribes, changed over time. To illustrate this concept, Snyder points to the story of the Westo Indians, a group originally from around Lake Erie, who spoke an Iroquoian language. They left the North in the middle of the 17th century, Snyder says, "probably because of Iroquois competition over guns and slaving," and moved to the Southeast, where they enslaved local Indians for sale to colonists. "But then the colonists got anxious, or they were afraid that this group was too powerful," Snyder said; in 1680, a group of Carolinians armed the Savannah Indians and empowered them to break the Westos' strength in the area. **The remaining Westos were, themselves, sold to the Caribbean as slaves**.

* * *

The many stories of Native slavery force us to think about the strategies Native people used to respond to the relentless European desire for labor. Some, like the Yamasee—who, with their allies, rose up to challenge British colonists in South Carolina in 1715-16—fought enslavement with violent resistance.

http://www.slate.com/articles/news_and_politics/cover_story/2016/01/native_american_slavery_historians_uncover_a_chilling_chapter_in_u_s_history.html

Native American slavery "is a piece of the history of slavery that has been glossed over," says Linford D. Fisher, associate professor of history at Brown University. "Between 1492 and 1880, between 2 and 5.5 million Native Americans were enslaved in the Americas...

While natives had been forced into slavery and servitude as early as 1636, it was not until King Philip's War that natives were enslaved in large numbers, Fisher writes in the study. The 1675 to 1676 war pitted Native American leader King Philip, also known as Metacom, and his allies against the English colonial settlers.

During the war, New England colonies routinely shipped Native Americans as slaves to Barbados, Bermuda, Jamaica, the Azores, Spain, and Tangier in North Africa, Fisher says.

While Africans who were enslaved did not know where they would be taken, Native Americans understood that they could be sent to Caribbean plantations and face extremely harsh treatment far from their homes and communities, according to the study. **Fear of this fate spurred some Native Americans to pledge to fight to the death, while others surrendered hoping to avoid being sent overseas**, the study found.

Fisher's study appears in the journal Ethnohistory. Documentation of Native American enslavement shows up in colonial correspondence, shipping records, court cases, town records, colonial government orders, and petitions from colonists to the British government.

"Even contemporary official histories of the war all point to the same thing: **Indians were enslaved en masse and either**

distributed locally or sent overseas to a variety of destinations," Fisher writes in the study.

Studies in native slavery have opened up in recent years, Fisher says, with award-winning books published in 2002 and 2003 highlighting the systematic nature of indigenous enslavement, even within English colonies. Fisher's study on those who surrendered in King Philip's War looks at what factors contributed to native slavery and the impact enslavement had on Native Americans for generations.

Fisher examines the short- and long-term effects of native slavery in his study, noting that during the war, the widespread fear of being sold overseas as slaves was used by Philip-allied Native Americans as a tool to recruit natives to their side.

Other Native Americans surrendered, Fisher writes, either in response to explicit inducements by the English offering mercy, or because they hoped that doing so would be understood as a statement of neutrality. These surrenderers could be individuals, families, larger bands, or entire communities, Fisher says.

Some Native Americans offered their services to the English in the war, like Awashonks, the female chief of a confederation of Sakonnet Indians, who pledged support on the condition that Sakonnet men, women and children would not be killed or sent out of the country as slaves, according to the study.

Especially near the war's end, Fisher writes, natives surrendered in larger numbers in direct response to promises of leniency, but "leniency" had no consistent, practical meaning.

English authorities focused first on disarming natives, either by selling guns turned in by surrenderers or prohibiting them from bearing arms, Fisher writes. English communities objected to letting natives who surrendered simply go free, and housing and feeding them was complicated, so often captured and surrendered Native Americans were simply sold into slavery, both overseas and within New England, or forced into servitude for limited terms within English households.

In addition, native communities were asked to pay an annual tribute of five shillings per male “as an acknowledgment of their subjection” to the government of Connecticut, according to the study.

New Englanders’ motivations for enslaving Native Americans included making money and clearing land for colonists to claim, Fisher writes. It was also easier to remove Native Americans from the region than to sell them locally and risk having the Native Americans run away to find refuge.

Fisher also argues that there was an ideological component to enslaving Native Americans. Among colonists, “there was a presumption involving the innate inferiority of natives,” he says.

“There were proto-racial notions of European superiority, plus an appetite for land,” he says. “If you look at the history of the colonies, slavery happens almost right away.”

Fisher says he is increasingly convinced that, for colonists, “slavery was a normal part of their mental framework.”

Some free Native Americans working with the English tried to influence where Native American surrenderers would be settled and how they would be treated, Fisher writes, like Uncas, the sachem of the Mohegans in Connecticut.

Uncas, who fought on the side of the English, “seemed determined postwar to keep Indians out of English households and—even more important—off of English merchant ships that threatened to take them to the Caribbean,” Fisher writes. Uncas and other Native Americans also encouraged captives to run away and sheltered them when they did, or helped them resettle elsewhere, according to the study.

In other cases, Fisher writes, Native Americans requested captives as servants for themselves, sometimes to keep them out of English households, or served as slave-trading middlemen. In one case, Fisher notes, a Native American slave owned by a Pequot leader was sold by him to an enslaved African woman.

"The shadow of native enslavement in New England extends into the 18th century and beyond," Fisher says. "There are records of people petitioning for freedom in the 1740s who were the descendants of Native Americans first enslaved during King Philip's War."

In the study, he writes, "**Small legal loopholes and dishonest practices on the ground ensured that, in many cases, limited-term service turned into lifelong and even heritable slavery**." In 1676, **Connecticut officials decreed that a native slave's term of service could be lengthened but not shortened**.

A law passed the same year by the Rhode Island General Assembly seemed on the surface to outlaw Indian slavery, but, Fisher notes, in practice that and other laws ensured that Native surrenderers were "disposed of" for the benefit of the colony, with various terms of servitude. **For Native Americans five years of age or younger, their servitude lasted until they were 30 years old**.

These enslavement practices permanently disrupted the "lives, livelihoods, and kinship networks of thousands of Indians," Fisher writes, **and sometimes slavery was simply given another name**.

In 1721, 45 years after the end of King Philip's War, the Connecticut General Assembly took up the question of second-generation Native American child slaves. The Native American children who had been placed as servants in English households after the war had grown up and had children of their own. What should be done with them? Fisher writes that while leaders did not approve of enslaving them, they also did not want to set them free, so that generation of children also became indentured servants.

Native Americans sold overseas occasionally made it back to the United States, Fisher writes. Others died or disappeared into a wider slave market and labor force, or became established in the locations where they were sent, like the modern-day community of individuals in Bermuda who claim New England Indian descent.

https://www.futurity.org/native-americans-slavery-1361262-2/

The historical record of the Indian slave trade is based on many disparate and scattered sources including legislative notes, trade transactions, journals of slavers, government correspondence and especially church records, making it difficult to account for the entire history. It is well known by historians that the slave trade began with the Spanish incursions into the Caribbean and Christopher Columbus's taking of slaves, as documented in his own journals. **Every European nation that colonized North America utilized Indian slaves for construction, plantations, and mining on the North American continent but more frequently in their outposts in the Caribbean and in the metropoles of Europe**.

As the pieces of the puzzle come together in the scholarship, historians note that nowhere is there more documentation than in South Carolina, what was the original English colony of Carolina, established in 1670. It is estimated that between 1650 and 1730

at least 50,000 Indians (and likely more due to transactions hidden to avoid paying government tariffs and taxes) were exported by the English alone to their Caribbean outposts. Between 1670 and 1717 far more Indians were exported than Africans were imported. **In southern coastal regions, entire tribes were exterminated through slavery compared to disease or war**. In a law passed in 1704, Indian slaves were conscripted to fight in wars for the colony long before the American Revolution.

The Indian slave trade covered an area **from as far west and south as New Mexico (then Spanish territory) northward to the Great Lakes**. Historians believe that all tribes in this vast swath of land were caught up in the slave trade in one way or another, either as captives or as traders. **Slavery was part of the larger strategy to depopulate the land to make way for European settlers**. (See my book on White Privilege) As early as 1636 after the Pequot war in which 300 Pequots were massacred, those who remained **were sold into slavery and sent to Bermuda. Major slaving ports included Boston, Salem, Mobile and New Orleans. From those ports Indians were shipped to Barbados by the English, Martinique and Guadalupe by the French and the Antilles by the Dutch. Indian slaves were also sent to the Bahamas as the "breaking grounds" where they might've been transported back to New York or Antigua**.

The historical record indicates a perception that Indians did not make good slaves. When they weren't shipped far from their home territories they too easily escaped and were given refuge by other Indians if not in their own communities. **They died in high numbers on the transatlantic journeys** and succumbed easily to European diseases. By 1676 Barbados had banned Indian slavery citing "too bloody and dangerous an inclination to remain here."

As the Indian slave trade gave way to the African slave trade by the late 1700's (by then over 300 years old) Native American women began to intermarry with imported Africans, **producing mixed-race offspring whose native identities became obscured through time. In the colonial project to eliminate the landscape of Indians, these mixed-race people simply became known as "colored" people through bureaucratic erasure in public records. In some cases such as in Virginia, even when people were designated as Indians on birth or death certificates or other public records, their records were changed to reflect "colored." Census takers, determining a person's race by their looks, often recorded mixed-race people as simply black, not Indian**. The result is that today there is a population of people of Native American heritage and identity (particularly in the Northeast) who are not recognized by society at large, sharing similar circumstances with the Freedmen of the Cherokee and other Five Civilized Tribes.

https://www.thoughtco.com/untold-history-of-american-indian-slavery-2477982

With labor at a premium in the colonial American economy, there was no shortage of people seeking to purchase slaves. **Both before and during African enslavement in the Americas, American Indians were forced to labor as slaves and in various other forms of unfree servitude**. They worked in mines, on plantations, as apprentices for artisans, and as domestics—just like African slaves and European indentured servants. As with Africans shipped to America, **Indians were transported from their natal communities to labor elsewhere as slaves. Many Indians from Central America were shipped to the West**

Indies, also a common destination for Indians transported out of Charleston, South Carolina, and Boston, Massachusetts. Many other Indians were moved hundreds or thousands of miles within the Americas. Sioux Indians from the Minnesota region could be found enslaved in Quebec, and Choctaws from Mississippi in New England. A longstanding line of transportation of Indian slaves led from modern-day Utah and Colorado south into Mexico.

The European trade in American Indians was initiated by Columbus in 1493. Needing money to pay for his New World expeditions, **he shipped Indians to Spain, where there already existed slave markets** dealing in the buying and selling of Africans. Within a few decades, the Spanish expanded the slave trade in American Indians from the island of Hispaniola to Puerto Rico, Jamaica, Cuba, and the Bahamas. The great decline in the indigenous island populations which largely owed to disease, slaving, and warfare, led the Spanish to then raid Indian communities in Central America and many of the islands just off the continent, such as Curacao, Trinidad, and Aruba. About 650,000 Indians in coastal Nicaragua, Costa Rica, and Honduras were enslaved in the sixteenth century. Conquistadors then entered the inland American continents and continued the process. Hernando de Soto, for instance, brought with him iron implements to enslave the people of La Florida on his infamous expedition through the American southeast into the Carolinas and west to the Mississippi Valley. Indians were used by the conquistadors as tamemes to carry their goods on these distant forays. Another form of Spanish enslavement of Indians in the Americas was yanaconaje, which was similar to European serfdom, whereby Indians were tied to specific lands to labor rather than lords. And under the encomienda system, Indians were forced to labor or pay tribute to an encomendero, who, in exchange, was supposed to provide protection and conversion to Christianity. The encomenderos' power survived longest in frontier areas, particularly in Venezuela, Chile, Paraguay, and in the Mexican Yucatan into the nineteenth century.

By 1542 the Spanish had outlawed outright enslavement of some, but not all, Indians. People labeled cannibals could still be enslaved, as could Indians purchased from other Europeans or from Indians. The Spanish also created new forms of servitude for Indians. This usually involved compelling mission Indians to labor for a period of time each year that varied from weeks to months with little or no pay. Repartimiento, as it was called, was widespread in Peru and Mexico, though it faded quickly in the latter. It persisted for hundreds of years as the main system for organizing Indian labor in Colombia, Ecuador, and Florida, and survived into the early 1820s in Peru and Bolivia. Indian laborers worked in the silver mines and built forts, roads, and housing for the army, church, and government. They performed agriculture and domestic labor in support of civilians, government contractors, and other elements of Spanish society. Even in regions where African slavery predominated, such as the sugar plantations in Portuguese Brazil and in the West Indies, Indian labor continued to be used. And in many Spanish colonies, where the plantations did not flourish, Indians provided the bulk of unfree labor through the colonial era. In other words, the growth of African slavery in the New World did not diminish the use of unfree Indian labor, particularly outside of the plantation system.

Whereas in South America and the islands of the West Indies, Europeans conducted the bulk of slaving raids against Indians, (except in Brazil, where bandeirantes of mixed blood were employed for slaving… North American Europeans did enslave Indians during wars, especially in New England (the Pequot War,

King Philip's War) and the southeast (the Tuscarora War, the Yamasee War, the Natchez War, just to name a few),... Colonists lured Indians to supply Indian slaves in exchange for trade goods and to obtain alliances with the Europeans and their Indian allies. Indians slaved against not only their enemies, but Indians they had never met. Many Indians recognized they had little choice but to become slavers. If they did not do the Europeans' bidding they could easily become victimized themselves. It was not unusual for peoples victimized by slaving to become slavers, and for those who had been slavers to become the object of raids.

Colonists participated in Indian slave trading to obtain capital. It was as if capital could be created out of thin air: one merely had to capture an Indian or find an Indian to capture another. In South Carolina, and to a lesser extent in North Carolina, Virginia, and Louisiana, **Indian slavery was a central means by which early colonists funded economic expansion**. In the late seventeenth and early eighteenth centuries, a frenzy of enslaving occurred in what is now the eastern United States. **English and allied Indian raiders nearly depopulated Florida of its American Indian population**. From 1670 to 1720 more Indians were shipped out of Charleston, South Carolina, than Africans were imported as slaves—and Charleston was a major port for bringing in Africans. The populous Choctaws in Mississippi were repeatedly battered by raiders, **and many of their neighboring lower Mississippi Valley Indians also wound up spending their lives as slaves on West Indies plantations**. Simultaneously, **the New England colonies nearly eliminated the Native population from southern New England through warfare, slaving, and forced removal**. The French in Canada and in Louisiana purchased many Indian slaves from their allies who swept through the Great Lakes region, the Missouri Country, and up into Minnesota. All the colonies engaged in slaving and in the purchase of Indian slaves.

Only in the colonial region of New York and Pennsylvania was slaving limited, in large part because the neighboring Iroquois assimilated into their societies many of those they captured instead of selling them to the Europeans—but the Europeans of those colonies purchased Indian slaves from other regions.

https://ap.gilderlehrman.org/essay/indian-slavery-americas

When we think of slavery in the New World we immediately think of the capture and sale of African slaves who were then transported to North America. But, he argues, there was another kind of slavery in the New World — "the other slavery" — **that predated and outlasted the African slave trade that was in many ways more fundamental**.

While the archaeological record suggests that slavery between tribes existed before the coming of Europeans, their arrival transformed it and made it so widespread as to leave no part of North America untouched. The "other slavery" shaped the shared history of Mexico and later the United States, and was so deeply entrenched that it was ignored. Because "it had no legal basis, it was never formally abolished like African slavery," the "other slavery" continued well into the 20th century.

Reséndez launches his thesis with a bang that might (and probably should) upset the most widely held idea about the colonization of the New World: That as bad as the Spanish, Portuguese and later the English were, most Indians died from diseases against which most had no immunity, which was no one's fault. It's the "no harm no foul" approach to colonization.

But if this were true, if disease was the culprit, wonders Reséndez, why is there no mention of any major disease, much less pandemics, in the New World until 1519, a full 25 years after Columbus first set down on Hispaniola?

According to Reséndez, the Spanish were well aware of disease at that time; they knew exactly what smallpox was and what it looked like, but they make no mention of it. He explains why smallpox was unlikely to cross the Atlantic: **Smallpox was endemic in the Old World, and the majority of Europeans had been exposed to it as children and those who survived had lifelong immunity**. European sailors and passengers were unlikely to have an active smallpox infection. **And if they did it would have been hard for smallpox to cross the ocean, a journey of five or six weeks during which time an infected passenger would have died or recovered**. The disease probably spread more slowly than previously thought.

Meanwhile, an institution was put in place almost immediately that had grave consequences for Indians in the New World: slavery.

Even if Indians did contract diseases against which they had no immunity (like Europeans did during the Plague) they would have (like the Europeans during the plague) rebounded within a few decades. The major difference between Indian and European populations was the fact that Indians were enslaved to work on gold mines and silver mines in alarming numbers beginning on Columbus' second voyage whereas Europeans were not.

By 1520 whole Caribbean islands had been depopulated — the inhabitants moved to gold mines in what is now the Dominican Republic. **Tens of thousands of Indians were worked to death even after the Spanish monarchy outlawed slavery**.

As his narrative moves to Mexico, New Mexico and parts north, at each place and phase of the "other slavery" he shows a masterful grasp of the history and an astonishing command of archival material in not a few languages. He also shows, with startling clarity, how even after slavery was outlawed by the Spanish and then the Mexican and the American governments, **those interested in profiting from the enterprise deployed a bouquet of legal terms and frameworks to continue the practice**.

The perpetrators of this regime included explorers such as Cortes (the owner of the largest number of slaves in Mexico), territorial governors of New Mexico and U.S. officials. **For many years white Southern colonists exported more Indians from the southeastern United States than they imported black slaves**. Conflicts, such as the Pueblo Revolt of 1680, were in large part spurred by the ceaseless capture and conscription of Indians from all over New Mexico for export to the silver mines of Mexico.

Reséndez doesn't spare the reader the shock of seeing a whole system of settlement, colonialism and capitalism that was built around the institution of the enslavement of Indians. And he includes some shocking instances of depravity and cruelty perpetrated in the New World in the name of crown and Christ. Nor does he omit the variations on that central theme as practiced by some tribes against others. In particular, Reséndez illustrates how the "horse empires" of the southern plains of the Comanche and Utes became dominant and expanded their territory and their control not just by mastering the horse but also by becoming the masters of less fortunate Indians around them, including the Paiute, Pueblo, Mexicans and Apache.

What is profound about Reséndez's argument isn't simply that there was a kind of slavery older, more widespread and more pernicious than African slavery (or that it continued longer) but that there is a clear and direct relationship between the two. "In 1865-1866," he writes, "southern states enacted the infamous Black Codes aimed at restricting the freedom of former slaves. Adopting tried-and-true tactics such as vagrancy laws, convict leasing, and debts, white southerners sought to nullify the provisions of the Thirteenth Amendment." The tactics he lists were pulled from the playbook that had kept Indians in servitude in the West and in Mexico long after slavery had been made illegal.

Lest this carefully researched and compelling book make readers feel bad about every aspect of the settlement of the New World, the conclusion should make us feel bad and think hard about our own times as well. The "old slavery" based on the legal ownership of certain racial groups had been, for quite some time, replaced with a kind of "new slavery" based less on race and without legal standing and more on economic vulnerability: mechanisms of control meant to deprive workers of their freedom in order to extract their labor.

Reséndez concludes, "the other slavery that affected Indians throughout the Western Hemisphere was never a single institution, but instead a set of kaleidoscopic practices suited to different markets and regions. The Spanish crown's formal prohibition of Indian slavery in 1542 gave rise to a number of related institutions, such as encomiendas, repartimientos, the selling of convict labor, and ultimately debt peonage....In other words, **formal slavery was replaced by multiple forms of informal labor coercion and enslavement that were extremely difficult to track, let alone eradicate**."

https://www.latimes.com/books/jacketcopy/la-ca-jc-native-american-slavery-20160505-snap-story.html

When Europeans arrived as colonists in North America, Native Americans changed their practice of slavery dramatically. Native Americans began selling war captives to Europeans rather than integrating them into their own societies as they had done before. As the demand for labor in the West Indies grew with the cultivation of sugar cane, **Europeans enslaved Native Americans for the Thirteen Colonies, and some were exported to the "sugar islands**." The British settlers, especially those in the southern colonies, purchased or captured Native Americans to use as forced labor in cultivating tobacco, rice, and indigo. Accurate records of the numbers enslaved do not exist. Scholars estimate tens of thousands of Native Americans may have been enslaved by the Europeans, being sold by Native Americans themselves or European men.

Slaves became a caste of people who were foreign to the English (Native Americans, Africans and their descendants) and non-Christians. The Virginia General Assembly defined some terms of slavery in 1705:

All servants imported and brought into the Country ... who were not Christians in their native Country ... shall be accounted and be slaves. All Negro, mulatto and Indian slaves within this dominion ... shall be held to be real estate. If any slave resists his master ... correcting such slave, and shall happen to be killed in such correction ... the master shall be free of all punishment ... as if such accident never happened.

— Virginia General Assembly declaration, 1705 [11]

Colonists found that Native American slaves could easily escape, as they knew the country. The wars cost the lives of numerous colonial slave traders and disrupted their early societies. The remaining Native American groups banded together to face the Europeans from a position of strength. Many surviving Native American peoples of the southeast strengthened their loose coalitions of language groups and joined confederacies such as the Choctaw, the Creek, and the Catawba for protection.

Native American women were at risk for rape whether they were enslaved or not; during the early colonial years, settlers were disproportionately male. They turned to Native women for sexual relationships. Both Native American and African enslaved women suffered rape and sexual harassment by male slaveholders and other white men.

The exact number of Native Americans who were enslaved is unknown because vital statistics and census reports were at best infrequent. Andrés Reséndez estimates that between 147,000 and 340,000 Native Americans were enslaved in North America, excluding Mexico. Linford Fisher's estimates 2.5 million to 5.5 million Natives enslaved in the entire Americas. Even though records became more reliable in the later colonial period, **Native American slaves received little to no mention, or they were classed with African slaves with no distinction**. For example, in the case of "Sarah Chauqum of Rhode Island", her master listed her as mulatto in the bill of sale to Edward Robinson, but she won her freedom by asserting her Narragansett identity.

Little is known about Native Americans that were forced into labor. Two myths have complicated the history of Native American slavery: that Native Americans were undesirable as servants, and that Native Americans were exterminated or pushed out after King Philip's War. The precise legal status for some Native Americans is at times difficult to establish, as involuntary servitude and slavery were poorly defined in 17th-century British America. Some masters asserted ownership over the children of Native American servants, seeking to turn them into slaves. The historical uniqueness of slavery in America is that European settlers drew a rigid line between insiders, "people like themselves who could never be enslaved", and nonwhite outsiders, "mostly Africans and Native Americans who could be enslaved". A unique feature between natives and colonists was that colonists gradually asserted sovereignty over the native inhabitants during the seventeenth century, ironically transforming them into subjects with collective rights and privileges that Africans could not enjoy. The West Indies developed as plantation societies prior to the Chesapeake Bay region and had a demand for labor.

In the Spanish colonies, the church assigned Spanish surnames to Native Americans and recorded them as servants rather than slaves. Many members of Native American tribes in the Western United States were taken for life as slaves. In some cases, courts served as conduits for enslavement of Indians, as evidenced by the enslavement of the Hopi man Juan Suñi in 1659 by a court in Santa Fe for theft of food and trinkets from the governor's mansion. In the East, Native Americans were recorded as slaves.

Slaves in Indian Territory across the United States were used for many purposes, from work in the plantations of the East, to guides across the wilderness, to work in deserts of the West, or as soldiers in wars. Native American slaves suffered from European diseases and inhumane treatment, and many died while in captivity.

European colonists caused a change in Native American slavery, as they created a new demand market for captives of raids. Especially in the southern colonies, initially developed for resource exploitation rather than settlement, colonists purchased or captured Native Americans to be used as forced labor in cultivating tobacco, and, by the eighteenth century, rice, and indigo. To acquire trade goods, Native Americans began selling war captives to whites rather than integrating them into their own societies. Traded goods, such as axes, bronze kettles, Caribbean rum, European jewelry, needles, and scissors, varied among the tribes, but the most prized were rifles. The English copied the Spanish and Portuguese: they saw the enslavement of Africans and Native Americans as a moral, legal, and socially acceptable institution; a rationale for enslavement was "just war" taking captives and using slavery as an alternative to a death sentence. The escape of Native American slaves was frequent, because they had a better understanding of the land, which African slaves did not. Consequently, the Natives who were captured and sold into slavery were often sent to the West Indies, or far away from their home. The first African slave on record was located in Jamestown. Before the 1630s indentured servitude was dominant form of bondage in the colonies, but by 1636 only Caucasians could lawfully receive contracts as indentured servants. The oldest known record of a permanent Native American slave was a native man from Massachusetts in 1636. By 1661 slavery had become legal in all of the 13 colonies**. Virginia would later declare that "Indians, Mulattos, and Negros to be real estate**", and in 1682 New York forbade African or Native American slaves from leaving their master's home or plantation without permission. Europeans also viewed the enslavement of Native Americans differently than the enslavement of Africans in some cases; a belief that Africans were "brutish people" was dominant. While both Native Americans and Africans were considered savages, Native Americans were romanticized as noble people that could be elevated into Christian civilization

The Pequot War of 1636 led to the enslavement of war captives and other members of the Pequot by Europeans, almost immediately after the founding of Connecticut as a colony. The Pequot thus became an important part of New England's culture of slavery. The Pequot War was devastating: the Niantic, Narragansett, and Mohegan tribes were persuaded into helping the Massachusetts, Connecticut, and Plymouth colonists massacre the Pequot, with at least 700 of the Pequot killed. Most enslaved Pequot were noncombatant women and children, with **court records indicating that most served as chattel slaves for life**. Some court records show bounties on runaway native slaves more than 10 years after the War. **What further aided the Indian slave trade throughout New England and the South was that different tribes didn't recognize themselves as members of the same race, dividing the tribes among each other**. The Chickasaw and Westos, for example, sold captives of other tribes indiscriminately so as to augment their political and economic power.

Furthermore, Rhode Island also participated in the enslavement of Native Americans, but records are incomplete or non-existent, making the exact number of slaves unknown. The New England governments would promise plunder as part of their payment, and commanders like Israel Stoughton viewed the right to claim Native American women and children as part of their due. Because of lack of records it can only be speculated if the soldiers demanded these captives as sexual slaves or solely as servants. Few colonial leaders questioned the policies of the colonies' treatment of slaves, but Roger Williams, who tried to maintain positive connections with the Narragansett, was conflicted. As a Christian he felt that identifiable Indian murderers "deserved death", but he condemned the murder of Native American women and children, though most of his criticisms were kept private. Massachusetts originally kept peace with the Native American tribes in the region, but that changed, and the enslavement of Native Americans became inevitable. Boston newspapers mention escaped slaves as late as 1750. In 1790 the United States census report indicated that the number of slaves in the state was 6,001, with an unknown proportion of Native Americans, but at least 200 were cited as half-breed Indians (meaning half African). Since Massachusetts took the advance in the fighting of the King Philip's War and the Pequot War; it is most likely the Massachusetts colony greatly exceeded that of either Connecticut or Rhode Island in the number of Native American slaves owned. New Hampshire was unique: it had very few slaves, and maintained a somewhat peaceful stance with various tribes during the Pequot War and King Philip's War. **Colonists in the South began to capture and enslave Native Americans for sale and export to the "sugar islands" such as Jamaica, as well as to northern colonies**. The resulting Native American slave trade devastated the southeastern Native American populations and transformed tribal relations throughout the Southeast. In the seventeenth and eighteenth centuries, the English at Charles Town (in modern South Carolina), the Spanish in Florida, and the French in Louisiana sought trading partners and allies among the Native Americans by offering goods such as metal knives, axes, firearms and ammunition, liquor, beads, cloth, and hats in exchange for furs (deerskins) and Native American slaves.

Traders, frontier settlers, and government officials encouraged Native Americans to make war on each other, to reap the profits of the slaves captured in such raids or to weaken the warring tribes. Starting in 1610, the Dutch traders had developed a lucrative trade with the Iroquois. The Iroquois gave the Dutch beaver pelts; in exchange the Dutch gave them clothing, tools, and firearms, which gave them more power than neighboring tribes had. The trade allowed the Iroquois to have war campaigns against other tribes, like the Eries, Huron, Petun, Shawnee, and the Susquehannocks. The Iroquois also began to take war captives and sell them. The increased power of the Iroquois, combined with the diseases the Europeans unknowingly brought, devastated many eastern tribes.

Indian slave trade in the American Southeast

Carolina, which originally included today's North Carolina, South Carolina, and Georgia, was unique among the North American English colonies because the colonists thought of slavery as essential to their success. In 1680, proprietors ordered the Carolina government to ensure that enslaved Native Americans had equal justice and to treat them better than African slaves; these regulations were widely publicized, so no one could claim ignorance of them. The change in policy in Carolina was rooted in fear that escaped slaves would inform their tribes, resulting in even more devastating attacks on plantations. The new policy proved almost impossible to enforce, **as both colonists and local officials viewed Native Americans and Africans as the same**, and the exploitation of both as the easiest way to wealth, though the proprietors continued to attempt to enforce the changes for profit reasons.

In the other colonies slavery developed into a predominant form of labor over time. It is estimated that Carolina traders operating out of Charles Town exported an estimated 30,000 to 51,000 **Native American captives between 1670 and 1715 in a profitable slave trade with the Caribbean, Spanish Hispaniola, and Northern colonies. It was more profitable to have Native American slaves because African slaves had to be shipped and purchased, while native slaves could be captured and immediately taken to plantations**; whites in the Northern colonies sometimes preferred Native American slaves, especially Native women and children, to Africans because Native American women were agriculturalist and children could be trained more easily. However, Carolinians had more of a preference for African slaves but also capitalized on the Indian slave trade combining both. In December 1675 Carolina's grand council created a written justification of the enslavement and sale of Native Americans, claiming that those who were enemies of tribes the English had befriended were targets, stating those enslaved were not "innocent Indians". The council also claimed it was within the wishes of their "Indian allies" to take their prisoners and that the prisoners were willing to work in the country or be transported elsewhere. The council used this to please the proprietors, and to fulfill the practice of enslaving no one against their wishes or be transported without his own consent out of Carolina, though this is what the colonists did.

In John Norris' "Profitable Advice for Rich and Poor (1712)", he recommended buying eighteen native women, fifteen African men, and three African women. **Slave traders preferred captive Native Americans who were under eighteen years old, as they were believed to be more easily trained to new work**. In the Illinois Country, French colonists baptized the Native American slaves whom they bought for labor. They believed it essential to convert Native Americans to Catholicism. Church baptismal records have thousands of entries for Indian slaves. In the eastern colonies it became common practice to enslave Native American women and African men with a parallel growth of enslavement for both Africans and Native Americans. This practice also lead to large number of unions between Africans and Native Americans. This practice of combining African slave men and Native American women was especially common in South Carolina. Native American women were cheaper to buy than Native American men or Africans. Moreover, it was more efficient to have native women because they were skilled laborers, the primary agriculturalists in their communities. During this era it wasn't uncommon for reward notices in colonial newspapers to mention runaway slaves speaking of Africans, Native Americans, and those of a partial mix between them.

Many early laborers, including Africans, entered the colonies as indentured servants and could be free after paying off their passage. Slavery was associated with people who were non-Christian and non-European.

And also be in [sic.] enacted, by the authority aforesaid, and **it is hereby enacted, That all servants imported and brought into the Country... who were not Christians in their native country, (except... Turks and Moors in amity with her majesty, and others that can make due proof of their being free in England, or any other Christian country, before they were shipped...) shall be accounted and be slaves, and such be here bought and sold notwithstanding a conversion to Christianity afterward.**

And if any slave resists his master, or owner, or other person, by his or her order, correcting such slave, and shall happen to be killed in such correction, it shall not be accounted felony; but the master, owner, and every such other person so giving correction, shall be free and acquit of all punishment and accusation for the same, as if such incident had never happened

In the mid-18th century, South Carolina colonial governor James Glen began to promote an official policy that aimed to create in Native Americans an "aversion" to African Americans in an attempt to thwart possible alliances between them. In 1758, James Glen wrote: "**It has always been the policy of this government to create an aversion in them Indians to Negroes**."

The dominance of the Native American slave trade lasted only until around 1730, when it led to a series of devastating wars among the tribes. The slave trade created tensions that were not present among different tribes and even large scale abandonment of original homelands to escape the wars and slave trade. The majority of the Indian wars occurred in the south. The Westos originally lived near Lake Erie in the 1640s but relocated to escape the Indian slave trade and Iroquois mourning wars designed to repopulate the Iroquois Confederacy due to European enslavement and large number of deaths due to wars and disease. The Westos eventually moved to Virginia and then South Carolina to take advantage of trading routes. The Westos strongly contributed to the rising involvement of southeastern Native American communities in the Indian slave trade especially with Westos expansion. The increased rise of the gun-slave trade forced the other tribes to participate or their refusal to engage in enslaving meant they would become targets of slavers. Before 1700, the Westos in Carolina dominated much of the Native American slave trade, enslaving natives of southern tribes indiscriminately. The Westos gained power rapidly but the British and plantation owners began to fear them as they were well-armed with a lot of rifle power through trading; unremorsefully from 1680 to 1682 the English, allied with the Savannah who resented Westo control of the trade wiped them out killing most of the men and selling most of the women and children that could be captured. As a result, **the Westo tribal group was completely eliminated culturally**; **its survivors were scattered or else sold into slavery in Antigua**. Those Native Americans nearer the European settlements raided tribes farther into the interior in the quest for slaves to be sold, especially to the British.

In response, the southeastern tribes intensified their warring and hunting, which increasingly challenged their traditional reasons for hunting or warring. The traditional reasoning for war was revenge not for profit. The Chickasaw war parties had pushed the Houmas tribe further south where the tribe struggled to find stability. In 1704, the Chickasaw alliance with the French had weakened and the British used the opportunity to make an alliance with the

Chickasaw bringing them 12 Taensa slaves. In Mississippi and Tennessee the Chickasaw played both the French and British against each other, and preyed on the Choctaw, who were traditional allies of the French, as well as the Arkansas, the Tunica, and the Taensa, establishing slave depots throughout their territories. In 1705, the Chickasaw activated their war parties again targeting the unexpected Choctaw since a friendship had been established between the two tribes; several Choctaw families were taken into captivity rekindling a war between the two tribes and ending their allegiance. A single Chickasaw raid in 1706 on the Choctaw yielded 300 Native American captives for the English. The warring between them continued through the early 18th century with the worse incident for the Choctaw occurring in 1711 as the British also attacked the Choctaw simultaneously fearing them more because of they were allies to the French. It is estimated that this warring mixed with enslavement and epidemics devastated the Chickasaw, it is estimated that in 1685 their population was 7,000 plus but by 1715 it was as low as 4,000. As the southern tribes continued their involvement in slave trade they became more involved economically and began to amass significant debts. The Yamasee amassed a great debt in 1711 for rum, but the General Assembly had voted to forgive their debts, but the tribe replied by stating they were preparing for war to pay their debts. The Indian slave trade began to negatively affect the social organization in many of the southern tribes particularly in gender roles in their communities. As male warriors began to interact more with colonial men and societies which were heavily patriarchal they began to increasingly sought out control over captives to trade with European men. Among the Cherokee the undermining of women's power began to create tensions among their communities e.g. warriors started to undermine women's power to determine when to wage war. In the Cherokee and other tribes' societies "war women" and "beloved women" were those who had proven themselves in battle, and were respected with vested privileges to decide what to do with captives. The incidents led warring women to dress as traders in effort to get captives before warriors. A similar pattern of friendly and then hostile relations among the English and Native Americans followed in the southeastern colonies.

For example, the Creek, a loose confederacy of many different groups who had banded together to defend themselves against slave-raiding, allied with the English and moved on the Apalachee in Spanish Florida, destroying them as a group of people in the quest for slaves. These raids also destroyed several other Florida tribes, including the Timucua. In 1685, the Yamasee were persuaded by Scottish slave traders to attack the Timucuans, the attack was devastating. Most of the colonial-era Native Americans of Florida were killed, enslaved, or scattered. It is estimated that English-Creek raids on Florida yielded 4,000 Native American slaves between 1700 and 1705. A few years later, the Shawnee raided the Cherokee in similar fashion. In North Carolina, the Tuscarora, fearing among other things that the English planned to enslave them as well as take their land, attacked the English in a war that lasted from 1711 to 1713. In this war, Carolina whites, aided by the Yamasee, completely vanquished the Tuscarora, taking thousands of captives as slaves. Within a few years, a similar fate befell the Yuchis and the Yamasee, who had fallen out of favor with the British. The French armed the Natchez tribe, who lived on the banks of the Mississippi, and the Illinois against the Chickasaw. By 1729, the Natchez, along with a number of enslaved and runaway Africans who lived among them, rose up against the French. An army composed of French soldiers, Choctaw warriors, and enslaved Africans defeated them. Trade behavior of several tribes also began to change returning to more traditional ways of adopting war captives instead of immediately selling them to white slave traders or holding them for three days before deciding to sell them or not. This was due to the heavy losses many of the tribes were obtaining in the numerous wars that continued throughout the 18th century.

The lethal combination of slavery, disease, and warfare dramatically decreased the free southern Native American populations; it is estimated that the southern tribes numbered around 199,400 in 1685 but decreased to 90,100 in 1715. The Indian wars of the early 18th century, combined with the growing availability of African slaves, essentially ended the Native American slave trade by 1750. Numerous colonial slave traders had been killed in the fighting, and the remaining Native American groups banded together, more determined to face the Europeans from a position of strength rather than be enslaved. During this time records also show that many Native American women bought African men but, unknown to the European sellers, the women freed and married the men into their tribe. Though the Indian slave trade ended the practice of enslaving Native Americans continued, records from June 28, 1771 show Native American children were kept as slaves in Long Island, New York. Native Americans had also married while enslaved creating families both native and some of partial African descent. Occasional mentioning of Native American slaves running away, being bought, or sold along with Africans in newspapers is found throughout the later colonial period. Many of the Native American remnant tribes joined confederacies such as the Choctaw, the Creek, and the Catawba for protection, making them less easy victims of European slavers. There are also many accounts of former slaves mentioning having a parent or grandparent who was Native American or of partial descent.

Records and slave narratives obtained by the WPA (Works Progress Administration) **clearly indicate that the enslavement of Native Americans continued in the 1800s mostly through kidnappings**. One example is a documented WPA interview from a former slave Dennis Grant whose mother was full blood Native American. She was kidnapped as a child near Beaumont, Texas in the 1850s, and made a slave later becoming a forced wife of a slave. **The abductions showed that even in the 1800s little distinction was still made between African Americans and Native Americans**. Both Native American and African-American slaves were at risk of sexual abuse by slaveholders and other white men of power. The pressures of slavery also gave way to the creation of colonies of runaway slaves and Native Americans living in Florida called Maroons.

https://en.wikipedia.org/wiki/Slavery_among_Native_Americans_in_the_United_States

Indians were enslaved in Virginia by settlers and traders from shortly after the founding of Jamestown until the end of the eighteenth century, peaking late in the seventeenth century and providing a workforce for English plantations and households. However, and in the meantime those white Virginians who required men and women to work as servants or in tobacco fields mostly relied on indentured servants and **enslaved Indians**. Europeans sold guns for slaves in an existing indigenous trading market, and encouraged allied tribes to provide the slaves by targeting Indian groups on the periphery of English settlements (similar to African participation in the capture of slaves in Africa). While there are examples of continued enslavement of Indians throughout the early settlement period, mass enslavement typically coincided with the upheaval of war that led to Indian prisoners who could be sold as slaves. Virginia's laws were neither clear nor effective with respect to the enslavement of Indians, at times banning the practice and at other times encouraging it. American Indians were most clearly deemed free by Virginia law early in the 1800s, and Indians who were unable to gain their freedom often became assimilated within the predominantly African slave communities.

Slavery, generally absent any modern conception of race, had long been common practice around the world and usually involved the enslavement of war captives. For centuries before European settlement, American Indian tribes had enslaved other Indians as a cultural practice—but not as a means of recruiting a dominant labor source. The Spanish, in turn, enslaved Indians to work on North American sugar plantations, using the repartimiento and encomienda systems to apportion Indians and land, and to govern their use, respectively. Only when **mistreatment decimated whole indigenous populations** did the Spanish government, in 1542, outlaw Indian slavery, at least in name. The practice continued in deed.

Neither the Spanish nor the English immediately sought to enslave the Indians they encountered. Indian slavery did not become official Spanish policy until 1503, or eleven years after first contact. It is clear that the English wanted to mimic Spanish efforts at creating indigenous tributaries for a labor force, but it took them even longer. The tributary relationship involved the exchange of Indian goods and labor for colonial protection against enemy tribes. Upon their arrival in 1607, the English initially sought to establish this kind of tributary trading relationship with the Algonquian-speaking Indians of Tsenacomoco, a paramount chiefdom of twenty-eight to thirty-two small chiefdoms and tribes stretching from the James to the Potomac rivers. The Indians had food the English needed and the English provided tools, weapons, fabric, and copper-made items the Indians considered to be spiritually valuable. Indians labored for the English as indentured servants without clearly defined rights or lengths of service. Conflict soon weakened such relationships.

An early mention of an Indian slave appears in the context of the First Anglo-Powhatan War (1609–1614). In his Trewe Relacyon, George Percy recounts an English march on an Indian town guided by an Indian named Kempes, who was "led in a hand locke" and is described as a slave working under the threat of beatings and beheading. The war, meanwhile, resulted in English expansion outside Jamestown, which helped create another use for forced Indian labor. With the subsequent development of tobacco as a cash crop came the need for an abundant and cheap labor supply to work the fields. Then, on March 22, 1622, Indians under the leadership of Opechancanough attacked settlements along the James River, killing nearly a third of the English population and initiating the Second Anglo-Powhatan War (1622-–1632). With the friendly tributary approach decaying, a new English policy toward the Indians was born of this violence and found expression in the official Virginia Company of London report of the 1622 attack, A Declaration of the state of the Colonie and Affaires in Virginia. Describing Virginia's Indians as "a rude, barbarous, and naked people" who worship the devil, the report's author argued that "the Indians who before were used as friends may now most justly be compelled to servitude and drudgery." As the historian C. S. Everett has explained, **the enslavement of Indians from 1610 to 1645 tended to be a form of "punitive retribution**."

Animosity and distrust was growing between the English and the Indians. Indians continued to provide labor under circumstances that, while legally unclear, often amounted to slavery. Everett has argued that deeds and wills from this time period indicate that Indians were inherited within white families and that they "were not indentured servants ... Indisputably, and by 1661 at the latest, Indians could be—and were—lifelong servants." In other words, **they were slaves**.

Only after the Third Anglo-Powhatan War (1644–1646) did Indian slavery become a lucrative part of the Virginia economy. The treaty ending the war defined the tribes and chiefdoms of Tsenacomoco as a tributaries and subject to English rule, requiring yearly payment to the crown and dictating where Indians could live, hunt, and trade. To coerce Indians to comply with the treaty, the English also demanded that Indian children "shall or will freely or voluntarily come in and live with the English"—serving as hostage-servants in English households. The English claimed they were educating and converting the children to Christianity as part of the tributary system, **but many Indians complained that these children were subsequently sold on the slave market**.

By 1649, **the enslavement of children in English households and the stealing of Indian children for the slave market was so common** that the General Assembly enacted two laws: one stipulating that no tributary children could be sold as slaves, the other that they could not be kept in households after the age of twenty-five. The assembly passed similar prohibitions in 1655, 1656, and in 1657, outlining punishments for anyone stealing and enslaving Indian children. Despite these laws, by the late seventeenth century many Indians refused to bring their children to English households due to the threat of enslavement. And even as Virginia prohibited the enslavement of Indian children, the government sometimes encouraged it. Officials in Accomack

County, for instance, on June 16, 1670, commissioned a man they called "Mr. John" to find Indian children to sell to the settlers.

Not only were children being enslaved after the 1646 treaty, but the treaty's provisions for English dominance led to the practice of enslaving Indians for legal violations and even as a means of financing war. For instance, when John Powell appealed to the General Assembly in 1660 for damages caused by Indians in Northumberland County, the assembly responded with a retribution act compensating him with the sale of Wicocomoco Indians, **who would be "apprehended and sold into a forraigne country**." The historian Edmund S. Morgan has explained that the casual nature of this act "speaks volumes" about the acceptability of enslaving Indians by this period.

Similarly in 1666, Governor Sir William Berkeley presided over the General Court and declared that hostilities with the **tribes of the Northern Neck be revenged by "utter destruction," and that taking "their women and children and their goods"—i.e., selling them—would compensate the colony for the costs of the expedition. Although a 1670 law indicated that captives should be servants who are freed at age thirty and not slaves bound to a lifetime of forced labor, the law was largely ignored**.

After 1646, **Indian labor was more common in many forms, from child hostages to indentured servants to slaves**. These enslaved Indians worked in the fields and as house servants, interpreters, hunters, and guides. English colonists preferred enslaved Indian women and children as domestic laborers, rather than African or white laborers, because they were considered easiest to train and control. Indian men were perceived to pose a greater risk of obstinacy and escape, and so they were often profitably sold to American buyers as far away as New England or

to the sugar plantations in the West Indies (where they could not escape). The historian Everett has argued that when these external markets became available, financial incentive overtook vengeance as the primary driver of Indian enslavement. When the English colonists began to participate in an existing Indian trade that involved slaves and guns, Indian enslavement briefly became an important part of the colonial economy.

By the middle of the seventeenth century, labor-intensive tobacco dominated the Virginia economy, requiring a large and steady workforce. In addition to mostly white indentured servants and African slaves, English colonists also relied on enslaved Indians. They were purchased often from other Indians, who captured their enemies and traded them to English dealers for English guns. Once some tribes began to be well-armed from the gun trade, others were often compelled to enter the market: if they didn't arm themselves with European weapons and enslave other Indians, they would themselves become targets of slavers. As the English increasingly wanted to trade for slaves, and Indians increasingly wanted to trade for guns, the market focused more on slaves while also becoming more violent.

Several Indian tribes became prominent slavers in Virginia, including the Ricahecrian tribe. Originally from the area around Lake Erie, in New York, the tribe had been displaced by the Iroquois during the Beaver Wars, a series of Indian conflicts during the mid-1600s. In 1656, the Ricahecrian Indians abandoned their settlements in New York and moved south, seeking trade at the falls of the James River in Henrico County. After settling in Virginia and becoming known as the Westo, they became feared raiders. Initially, Colonel Edward Hill was charged by the General Assembly with nonviolently removing the Westo Indians from the region. However, Hill's militia, aided by

Pamunkey and Chickahominy forces, fought the Westo at the Battle of Bloody Run (1656), in Richmond, which resulted in the death of Totopotomoy, weroance, or chief, of the Pamunkey. The assembly subsequently suspended Hill and charged him with paying for an agreement of peace with the tribe. The Westo then secured arrangements with English traders to barter guns for slaves. The colony was less concerned with forcing the Westo Indians into tributary status and more interested in profitable trade.

The Westo built an arsenal and began overpowering local tribes in Virginia and North Carolina, enslaving captives for the marketplace. The trade was so successful that, by late 1656, the Westo had expanded their influence, moved farther south out of Virginia to the Savannah River (in what would become Georgia), and began raiding as far south as the Spanish mission towns in the Florida. They raided communities, killing and enslaving for the English market. By 1659, the Spanish reported that these raiders were armed with guns and assisted by traders from Jamestown, such as the preeminent English trader Abraham Wood, who fed the newly enslaved Indians into the Virginia marketplace. In early 1662, Governor Berkeley placed Wood in charge of all trade with Indians like the Westo.

When the Westo vacated their place on the Virginia Piedmont trading path, members of the Occaneechi tribe, living on the falls of the Roanoke River, established themselves as the dominant Indian slave brokers in Virginia. As this trade in guns and slaves became larger and more profitable, conflict among tribes increased. Violence erupted on small and large scales. In 1670, for instance, Occaneechi Indians responded to Westo raids, killing Westo Indians aligned with Wood. The Westo and the Occaneechi raids spurred tribal conflict throughout the entire

Southeast, and many Indians were killed, enslaved, or otherwise scattered.

https://www.encyclopediavirginia.org/indian_enslavement_in_virginia#start_entry

The Aboriginal American (Indian) Problem and Civilizing The Savage

By the 1880s, Indian reservations were interfering with western expansion, and many Americans felt that the only solution to the "**Indian Problem**" **was assimilation of Native Americans into Euro-American society**. The Government set a dramatic new policy under the Dawes Act dissolving tribal ownership of reservations into individual allotments for Native American ownership.

The policy was designed to force assimilation by separating Native Americans from their tribal affiliations and turning them into farmers, and eventually American citizens. Many Native Americans resisted farming because it conflicted with their traditional way of life. Most Native Americans also did not become citizens through the Dawes Act. However, the policy was immensely successful at opening up the West—divesting tribes of two-thirds of all remaining reservation lands.

http://recordsofrights.org/events/54/a-solution-to-the-indian-problem

The point that is forgotten in this whole mess is that the Aboriginal American was already a citizen. It was the Europeans, who were immigrants. How ironic is that? Foreigners telling people in their own homeland that they were not citizens.

On March 3, 1819, the United States Congress enacted the Civilization Fund Act, authorizing the President, **"in every case**

where he shall judge improvement in the habits and condition of such Indians practicable" to "employ capable persons of good moral character" to introduce to any tribe adjoining a frontier settlement the "arts of civilization."

With a budget of $10,000 per year, **the fund paid missionaries and church leaders to partner with the federal government to establish schools in Indian territories to teach Native children to replace tribal practices with Christian practices**. In 1824, **the federal government established the Bureau of Indian Affairs to oversee the fund and implement programs to "civilize" the Native people**.

In the following years, as **the United States systematically removed tribes from their homelands to land west of the Mississippi River, the United States turned to policies purportedly aimed at achieving "the great work of regenerating the Indian race."**

According to Indian Commissioner Luke Lea, **it was "indispensably necessary that they be placed in positions where they can be controlled, and finally compelled by stern necessity...until such time as their general improvement and good conduct may supersede the necessity of such restrictions**." **Over the ensuing decades, the United States' orientation to Native peoples changed from adversarial to paternalistic, focused on killing Native American culture**.

https://calendar.eji.org/racial-injustice/mar/03

The Civilization Fund Act was an Act passed by the United States Congress on March 3, 1819. The Act encouraged activities of benevolent societies in providing education for Native Americans and authorized an annuity to stimulate the **"civilization process"**. Thomas L. McKenney lobbied the Congress in support of the legislation. The Civilization Fund Act led to the formation of numerous Native American boarding schools towards the end of the 19th century.

The benevolent societies were a combination of Christian missions and the federal government.

Federal funds were allocated to schools designed to educate Native Americans in the ways of the white man. The goal was to "civilize" Native Americans by getting rid of their traditions and customs and teaching them reading and writing in the missionary schools.

The passage of the Act helped define a class structure within Native American society. While traditional Native Americans opposed the schools, "progressive" ones accepted the schools. **Their education and command of the English language propelled them to leadership positions within tribes and ultimately led to policy shifts and treaties that ceded land to the United States government.**

"That for the purpose of guarding against the further decline and final extinction of the Indian tribes, adjoining the frontier settlements of the United States, are for introducing among them the habits and arts of civilization" annual sum/annuity is ten thousand dollars "and an account of the expenditure of the money, and proceedings in execution of the foregoing provisions, shall be laid annually before Congress."

The Bureau of Indian Affairs was created in 1824 by the federal government and placed into the War Department. It was created in order to administer the annuity given to the schools.

https://en.wikipedia.org/wiki/Civilization_Fund_Act

In 1818, **James Monroe had come to believe that "independent savage communities" could no longer exist within the "civilized population" of the United States**. That is **he believed that if the United States did not take complete control of the Indian tribes and "civilize them", they would become extinct**. (Side note, How did they survive and not become extinct before the arrival of the European?) **Today, these are hard words to read because it sounds like he is talking about a herd of buffalo who may go extinct if not put in the security and seclusion of a refuge zone**. Did James Monroe believe that the Native American race was less superior, and thus needed the protection of the United States. No, rather, Monroe believed that the nomadic hunting culture of the Indian tribes was inferior to the Agricultural and Community-based culture of the United States. These were teachings that went back to the works of John Locke, one of the greatest minds of the Enlightenment period. It had it's roots in the Biblical teachings of "subduing the earth", that is make greatest use of the land to support the greatest number of people. It was the common belief of our founding fathers, and starting with Thomas Jefferson, then Madison and now Monroe, each had pushed policies to "civilize" the Indians. In this spirit, Monroe was now requesting that Congress consider "some benevolent provisions" for those "tribes within our settlements". That is, those tribes which had not yet been forced out. In Monroe's 1818 State of the Union address, he wrote these words:

"Experience has clearly demonstrated that independent savage communities can not long exist within the limits of a civilized population. The progress of the latter has almost invariably terminated in the extinction of the former, especially of the tribes belonging to **our** portion of this hemisphere, among whom loftiness of sentiment and gallantry in action have been conspicuous. **To civilize them, and even to prevent their extinction**, it seems to be indispensable that their independence as communities should cease, and that the control of the United States over them should be complete and undisputed. The hunter state will then be more easily abandoned, and recourse will be had to the acquisition and culture of land and to other pursuits tending to dissolve **the ties which connect them together as a savage community** and to give a new character to every individual. I present this subject to the consideration of Congress on the presumption that it may be found expedient and practicable to adopt some benevolent provisions, having these objects in view, relative to the tribes within our settlements."

http://www.stateoftheunionhistory.com/2017/04/1818-james-monroe-indian-civilization.html

How arrogant, dismissive and pompous does a person or society need to be? He states that it is "our" hemisphere when Europeans are not indigenous to it. They have no claim to it. They used the flawed and fraudulent Doctrine of Discovery to make their claim to it.

Congress responded in 1819 by approving $10,000 annually for Indian education under the Indian Civilization Act, also known as the Civilization Fund Act. The act was passed on march 3, 1819 to encourage benevolent **societies to provide education for the Indian tribes and provided the authorization to encourage the civilization programs**. The act led to the formation of 52 schools over the next decade which **were administered either by the federal government or by Christian missions**. (Separation of church and state) It was Monroe's hope that rather than forcibly remove the "savages" from the civilization of the United States, he could teach them to become part of it. Unfortunately, by time Monroe left office in 1825 he had reluctantly embraced forced removal and in a special message to Congress recommended that all Indians be removed and relocated west of the Mississippi.

Below is a short time line of previous words and initiatives of the previous 30 years.

1786 - Thomas Jefferson wrote in a letter to Benjamin Hawkins, that "The two principles on which our conduct towards the Indians should be founded are justice and fear. After the injuries we have done them, they cannot love us, which leaves us no alternative but that of fear to keep them from attacking us."

1801 - Thomas Jefferson introduced the Indian "Civilization Program", by that he meant to turn them away from the hunting and nomadic ways to the practice of "husbandry and household arts"

1813 - James Madison - When the British provoked the Indians into war against the U.S. Madison suggested we had to "chastise the savages into present peace but make a lasting impression on their fears"

1816 - James Madison suggested that it was now the time to complete the work of transitioning the Indians from the "habits of the savage to the arts and comforts of social life". This included, the ownership of property. In exchange for the millions of acres of hunting grounds, the United States would grant the Indians thousands of acres of farmland and protection.

1817 - James Monroe shared the progress that has been made in the "preservation, improvement, and civilization of the native inhabitants". Recent treaties were "were made with a view to individual ownership among them and to the cultivation of the soil by all, and that an annual stipend has been pledged to supply their other wants" http://www.stateoftheunionhistory.com/2017/04/1818-james-monroe-indian-civilization.html

The Treaty of Ghent ending the War of 1812 meant that Native American tribes could no longer turn to European nations in alliances against the United States. Although fighting would continue for many years, the eventual subjugation **of Native Americans had become all but a foregone conclusion. The government thus turned its emphasis in 1819 from military action to a "civilization policy" in which Native Americans would be taught basic education, religious training, and farming methods consistent with white, Christian principles**. The government allocated a relatively paltry $10,000 per year for this purpose, which was largely used for Christian missionary training. Most tribes did not embrace this policy. One exception was the Cherokee nation in the Southeast which cleared fields, established villages, learned trades, and went to schools and churches in significant numbers. Ironically, the success of the Cherokees contributed to their demise.

Eager to confiscate their fertile farms, President Andrew Jackson removed the Cherokees in the 1830s in a forced march westward. Be it enacted, etc., That, for the purpose of providing against the further decline and final extinction of the Indian tribes, adjoining to the frontier settlements of the United States, and for introducing among them the habits and arts of civilization, the President of the United States shall be, and he is hereby, authorized, in every case where he shall judge improvements in the habits and condition of such Indians practicable, and that the means of instruction can be introduced with their own consent, to employ capable persons, of good moral character, to instruct them in the mode of agriculture suited to their situation; and for teaching their children in reading, writing, and arithmetic, and for performing such other duties as may be enjoined, according to such instruction and rules as the President may give and prescribe for the regulation of their conduct, in the discharge of their duties....

From Our Nation's Archive: The History of the United States in Documents

https://mrsbraman.files.wordpress.com/2017/08/indian-civilization-act-of-1819.pdf

Compulsory Education

Native American boarding schools also known as, **Indian Residential Schools were established in the United States during the late 19th and mid 20th centuries with a primary objective of assimilating Native American children and youth into Euro-American culture, while at the same time providing a basic education in Euro-American subject matters**. These boarding schools were first established by Christian missionaries of various denominations, who often started schools on reservations, especially in the lightly populated areas of the West. **The government paid religious orders to provide basic education to Native American children on reservations**. In the late 19th and early 20th centuries, with the last residential schools closing as late as **1973**. the Bureau of Indian Affairs (BIA) founded additional boarding schools based on the assimilation model of the off-reservation Carlisle Indian Industrial School.

Children were typically immersed in European-American culture through forced changes that removed indigenous cultural signifiers. These methods included **being forced to have European-American style haircuts**, **being forbidden to speak their Indigenous languages**, **and having their real names replaced by European names to both "civilize" and**

"Christianize" them. The experience of the schools was usually harsh and sometimes deadly, especially for the younger children who were forcibly separated from their families. The children were forced to abandon their Native American identities and cultures. Investigations of the later twentieth century have revealed many documented cases of sexual, manual, physical and mental abuse occurring mostly in church-run schools.

https://en.wikipedia.org/wiki/American_Indian_boarding_schools

Beginning with the Indian Civilization Act Fund of March 3, 1819 and the Peace Policy of 1869 the United States, in concert with and at the urging of several denominations of the Christian Church, adopted an Indian Boarding School Policy expressly intended to **implement cultural genocide** through the removal and reprogramming of American Indian and Alaska Native children **to accomplish the systematic destruction of Native cultures and communities**. The stated purpose of this policy was to **"Kill the Indian, Save the Man."**

Between 1869 and the 1960s, it's likely that hundreds of thousands of Native American children were removed from their homes and families and placed in boarding schools operated by the federal government and the churches. Though we don't know how many children were taken in total, by 1900 there were 20,000 children in Indian boarding schools, and by 1925 that number had more than tripled. **The U.S. Native children that were voluntarily or forcibly removed from their homes, families, and communities during this time were taken to schools far away where they were punished for speaking their native language, banned from acting in any way that might be seen to represent traditional or cultural practices, stripped of traditional clothing, hair and personal belongings and**

behaviors reflective of their native culture. **They suffered physical, sexual, cultural and spiritual abuse and neglect**, **and experienced treatment that in many cases constituted torture for speaking their Native languages**. Many children never returned home and their fates have yet to be accounted for by the U.S. government.

https://boardingschoolhealing.org/education/us-indian-boarding-school-history/

All this ugliness was under the guise of civilizing the so-called Indian. It was from the perspective of we (European Christians) are and know what's better for these people than they know for themselves. The question arises again, how did the Aboriginal American fare for so long without the interference of the European? There society was fine for them. What cannot be ignored is the psychopathic thinking of the time.

This thinking wasn't just the leaders imposing inhumane conditions upon a free indigenous people. It was society as a whole. Everyone seemed to have one mind in agreement with the treatment of Aboriginal Americans. **None of these people had any authority to impose anything**. **They used brute force and deception to accomplish their demonic acts**. Then hid behind 'God', as further justification.

All of this has psychopathic and sociopathic tendencies. When looking at symptoms of sociopathic behavior, the results are startling.

Glibness and superficial charm. The ability to talk smooth but the talk is insincere. We can see this by all the treaties and promises that were broken. Manipulative and conning. "They never recognize the rights of others and see their self-serving behaviors as permissible." "They appear to be charming, yet are covertly hostile and domineering, seeing their victim as merely an instrument to be used." We see this applied by Europeans using the Aboriginal American whenever however they pleased. They would outlaw slavery, then turn around and ignore their own policies.

Grandiose sense of self, they "feel entitled to certain things as "their right." The mind state that says God told us to do this. Or God prefers for us to do this. We can see this in the Doctrine of Discovery and in Manifest Destiny.

Pathological lying "has no problem lying coolly and easily and it is almost impossible for them to be truthful on a consistent basis." We've seen this repeatedly.

Lack of remorse, shame or guilt, "does not see others around them as people, but only as targets and opportunities." This is dismissed as forgiveness in Christianity. They don't have to deal with their guilt or shame. Jesus removes it. "Instead of friends, they have victims and accomplices who end up as victims. The end always justifies the means and they let nothing stand in their way."

Shallow emotions, "when they show what seems to be warmth, joy, love and compassion it is more feigned than experienced and serves an ulterior motive." "Outraged by insignificant matters, yet remaining unmoved and cold by what would upset a normal person. Since they are not genuine, neither are their promises." Nothing else needs to be said about this.

Incapacity for love can be seen very clearly. Despite, Jesus is love, they showed no capacity to because of the harsh inhumane treatment of Aboriginal Americans.

Callousness/lack of empathy, "is demonstrated by the inability to empathize with the pain of their victims, having only contempt for others' feelings of distress and readily taking advantage of them."

Irresponsibility/unreliability "not concerned about wrecking others' lives and dreams. Oblivious or indifferent to the devastation they cause. Does not accept blame themselves, but blames others, even for acts they obviously committed."

Irresponsibility/unreliability "not concerned about wrecking others' lives and dreams. Oblivious or indifferent to the devastation they cause. Does not accept blame themselves, but blames others, even for acts they obviously committed."

Promiscuous sexual behavior/infidelity "promiscuity, child sexual abuse, rape and sexual acting out of all sorts." We can see this played out in all the raping of Aboriginal American women, also in the Indian boarding schools in regards to the children.

Lack of realistic life plan/parasitic "lifestyle tends to move around a lot or makes all encompassing promises for the future, poor work ethic but exploits others effectively."

https://www.mcafee.cc/Bin/sb.html

In Indian civilization I am a Baptist, because I believe in immersing the Indian in our civilization and when we get them under, holding them there until they are thoroughly soaked. —Richard Henry Pratt, founder of the Carlisle Indian Industrial School (Battlefield and Classroom: Four Decades with the American Indian, 1867-1904 by Richard Henry Pratt, 1964)

Indian boarding schools were founded to eliminate traditional American Indian ways of life and replace them with mainstream American culture. The first boarding schools were set up either by the government or Christian missionaries.

Initially, **the government forced many Indian families to send their children to boarding schools**. Later, Indian families chose to send their children because there were no other schools available.

At boarding schools, **Indian children were separated from their families and cultural ways for long periods, sometimes four or more years.** The children were forced to cut their hair and give up their traditional clothing. **They had to give up their meaningful Native names and take English ones. They were not only taught to speak English, but were punished for speaking their own languages**. **Their own traditional religious practices were forcibly replaced with Christianity**. **They were taught that their cultures were inferior. Some teachers ridiculed and made fun of the students' traditions. These lessons humiliated the students and taught them to be ashamed of being American Indian**. The boarding schools had a bad effect on the self-esteem of Indian students and on the well being of Native languages and cultures.

https://americanindian.si.edu/education/codetalkers/html/chapter3.html

Two centuries ago, Congress passed a law that kicked into high gear the U.S. government's campaign to assimilate Native Americans to Western culture—to figuratively "kill the Indian," as one general later put it, and "save the man."

The Civilization Fund Act of 1819, passed 200 years ago this week, had the purported goal of infusing the country's indigenous people with "**good moral character**" (as if they had it) and vocational skills. The law tasked Christian missions and the federal government with teaching young indigenous Americans subjects ranging from reading to math, eventually leading to a network of boarding schools designed to carry out this charge.

The act was, in effect, an effort to stamp out America's original cultural identity and replace it with one that Europeans had, not long before, imported to the continent. Over time, countless Native American children were taken from their families and homelands and placed in faraway boarding schools, a process that was often **traumatic and degrading**.

The Civilization Fund Act stressed that the boarding schools were only to enroll Native students whose families gave their consent. But as the novelist and historian David Treuer notes in his latest book, The Heartbeat of Wounded Knee: Native America From 1890 to the Present, **government workers often coerced Native parents through police seizures and threats**. Many others surrendered their kids to these institutions simply because they lacked a better alternative—perhaps they were so destitute that the schools, **where child labor and malnourishment were rampant**, felt like an improvement. It wasn't until the late 1970s that Congress outlawed the forced removal of Native children from their families. "The full effect of the boarding school system wouldn't be understood until decades after the agenda of 'civilizing the savage' ground down," writes Treuer, a member of the Minnesota Chippewa Tribe's Ojibwe band who was raised largely on the Leech Lake Indian Reservation.

https://www.theatlantic.com/education/archive/2019/03/failed-assimilation-native-american-boarding-schools/584017/

"It's a hidden part of American history," says Trafzer, a professor of American Indian History at the University of California-Riverside who began working with the school, now Sherman Indian High School, in 1991. "**Few people know about the boarding school system and the United States government taking children and bringing them to these schools,**

separating them from their families and their communities on purpose."

Many of the photos show students learning practical skills, such as sewing, smithing, or shoemaking. Those that appear staged, Trafzer says, were typically used by administrators to lobby for more federal funding.

"Yes, they were teaching English, a little bit of math and science, **but the emphasis was on making it a trade school—to make Native Americans useful**," he says. "To make them part of broader society. It was part of the assimilation program of the United States, **to totally change them**. **That's what we're seeing. An attempt to destroy that which was Indian and re-create people in the image of White America.**"

https://www.motherjones.com/media/2017/10/native-american-boarding-schools-shadows-of-sherman-institute/

How and why isn't this behavior on the part of invading Europeans not seen as psychopathic and sociopathic?

President Ulysses S. Grant advances a "Peace Policy" to remove **corrupt Indian agents**, who supervise reservations, and replace them with Christian missionaries, whom he deems morally superior.

"In reality the [peace] policy rested on the belief that **Americans had the right to dispossess Native peoples of their lands, take away freedoms, and send them to reservations, where missionaries would teach them how to farm, read and write, wear Euro-American clothing, and embrace Christianity**. If Indians refused to move to reservations, they would be forced off their homelands by soldiers." —Clifford Trafzer, ed., American Indians/ American Presidents: A History, 2009 https://www.nlm.nih.gov/nativevoices/timeline/342.html

We were taught in history and social studies classes that Europeans 'discovered' America as explorers, when they really were exploiters. The conquistadors were conquerors. They had the backing of the universal Christian church (Catholics) and their leaders the popes. They came under the fraudulent Doctrine of Discovery, which instructed them to accomplish exactly what they did. Their marching orders came from their Christian leaders. However, none of their acts were Christian. And continue to be justified in mainstream society.

Europeans invaded and did whatever they wanted. They made up the rules as they went along and changed them conveniently to suit whatever their needs were. This was the real Aboriginal American (Indian) problem. They existed for thousands of years before and without European influence.

www.ingramcontent.com/pod-product-compliance
Ingram Content Group UK Ltd.
Pitfield, Milton Keynes, MK11 3LW, UK
UKHW051136260726
13967UKWH00010B/3079